Pisanki (Easter Eggs)

Only to scratch the surface has its own integrity;
besides, a pattern is easier to comprehend than eggshells.

GW00391437

THE EMMA PRESS

small press, big dreams

The Emma Press is an independent publisher dedicated to producing beautiful, thought-provoking books. It was founded in 2012 by Emma Wright in Winnersh, UK, and is now based in Birmingham. Having been shortlisted in both 2014 and 2015, the Emma Press won the Michael Marks Award for Poetry Pamphlet Publishers in 2016.

The Emma Press is passionate about making poetry welcoming and accessible. In 2015 they received a grant from Arts Council England to travel around the country with *Myths and Monsters*, a tour of poetry readings and workshops for children. They are often on the lookout for new writing and run regular calls for submissions to their themed poetry anthologies and poetry pamphlet series.

Sign up to the monthly Emma Press newsletter to hear about their events, publications and upcoming calls for submissions. Their books are available to buy from the online shop, as well as in bookshops.

theemmapress.com

emmavalleypress.blogspot.co.uk/

Pisanki

By Zosia Kuczyńska

With an introduction by
Bernard O'Donoghue

THE EMMA PRESS

i.m. Maria Juralewicz (z domu Sztela)

ⳤ

THE EMMA PRESS

First published in Great Britain in 2017 by the Emma Press Ltd

Poems copyright © Zosia Kuczyńska 2017
Introduction copyright © Bernard O'Donoghue 2017

ISBN 978-1-910139-72-1

A CIP catalogue record of this book
is available from the British Library.

Printed and bound in Great Britain
by Charlesworth Press, Wakefield.

The Emma Press
theemmapress.com
queries@theemmapress.com
Birmingham, UK

Introduction

The backstory to Zosia Kuczyńska's haunting poems in *Pisanki* is a remarkable one: the removal of over 2000 Polish children to Maharashtra in India in 1942, after they and their families were deported to Siberia following the Soviet attack on Poland in 1939. Zosia Kuczyńska's grandmother, Maria Juralewicz (neé Sztela), was one of those redeemed children, and these poems draw on her recorded memories of that extraordinary experience as the displaced children travelled first from Russia to Persia, then to Karachi and on to Valivade. In 1948 Maria came to England with her sister and brother. This extraordinary odyssey is the context for *Pisanki*, which is dedicated to the memory of Maria Juralewicz.

But the odyssey is only the material of these remarkable poems; Kuczyńska weaves a wonderful tapestry of lyric poems out of it. Near the beginning of the collection, 'Fellow Traveller 2' is named after Sputnik 2, the first spacecraft to carry a living animal into orbit. At the other end of the book, 'Vespertiliones' draws on the story in Book 4 of Ovid's *Metamorphoses* in which the daughters of Minyas are turned into bats after disobeying the command of Bacchus to stop their work of weaving. Between these defining poems the book centres on two major themes: women's activities and experiences, and the ideas of home that the central section of the book turns on. One of the activities that women will not forego here is, as in Ovid, weaving: the final poem is 'On Hosiery', linking Chinese silk-making and the silk stockings that became the classic love-gift in the 'stocking-shortaged Blitz' with the Polish Easter practice of decorating eggs that gives the book its title. But there are other activities too: 'Wycinanki', Polish paper-cutting; storytelling; gardening – all the arts of home-making.

What it amounts to is 'the way you think of home' ('Sarah Jane's Geranium'), which of course links vitally to the desperate search for home of the displaced children in the 1940s. The search is finally successful: one of the most beautiful poems is 'Rochdale Nativity', celebrating the norms that have been achieved in the new home. But the journey's search for home is, after all, the unforgettable theme: the train which was the refugees' desperate temporary domicile, from which the women go out under cover of night to steal flour and other food, and, on one occasion, find the box they take is full of pistols: 'Midas died of hunger', as the poem about this inedible contraband remarks.

This altogether remarkable and accomplished book is indeed a text for the times, in this terrible epoch of failed refugees. But what it leaves us with is a sense of the triumph of the human spirit in the most adverse conditions. It does this without ever preaching, but by finding what Yeats called 'befitting emblems of adversity' in order to overcome it. It is a major and important achievement.

Bernard O'Donoghue
JANUARY 2017

Contents

The train from Arkhangelsk to Bukhara

Imagine the surprise of discovering pistols! They were all flung out through the open window into the fields.

—Maria Juralewicz (z domu Sztela)

You wake to find your field is sown with metal,
as though an artist had labelled it in the night
with the knowing title, *Midas died of hunger.*
Your land is crossed with trains of would-be flour-
thieves being carried to a landlocked sea.
Their children rattle inside their skins like guns
in looted crates, and anything they steal
that can't be swallowed is given to the view.
With the notable exception of the sea,
call nothing beautiful glimpsed from a moving train,
because a train is always running through it.

Brother Staś

I.

Between Drohiczyn and Tehran
is Arkhangelsk and, of course, the train.
It is nineteen forty-two.
Your parents' graves are smaller

than telegraph poles and as indistinct
from other parents' graves
as telegraph poles from telegraph poles
or breadcrumbs from breadcrumbs.

When you cross the Caspian Sea
to Pahlavi and Tehran,
your sister and brother
do not succumb to typhoid.

As for me I find, in fever dreams, the body
takes on qualities of darkened rooms,
all grain and grit and endless motes,
the white noise of scattered gravel

on woodland paths clever with brothers
who know the way back home.
And indeed it must have seemed
as though you were a stone

when you woke, an only child among lost children
so left behind that the backs of their sisters
and brothers moving on from sickness
were fantasies opulent as gingerbread houses.

II.

Unadorned for the miraculous,
a boiled egg cools to the heat of Easter in Tehran.
It is nineteen forty-two.
Hunger and convalescence have made you slight:

you juggle and peel,
and with the heatproof teeth of a fire-eater
reveal the improbable marigold
of a new life bashful with his acts of kindness;

you step from the crawling tent into the heart
of a white-hot day in which your brother,
unadorned for the miraculous,
appears.

III.

Between Tehran and Marigold Street
is Valivade and, of course, the sea.
HMT Asturias is, apparently,
a woman just like you,

and can no more imagine her final days
as RMS Titanic
in the film *A Night to Remember*
than you can imagine your brother

leaving England for New England,
or your brother flying home
to Marigold Street, the family saint,
growing another heart in his old man's head.

It is nineteen forty-eight.
You are yet to fall in love
with cups of tea;
when your daughter comes

to redefine him, he will give
your English neighbours rationed leaves
for powdered egg; he will become
an uncle the way a ship survives

its maiden voyage only to be repurposed,
flooded and abandoned
and refitted as the ship that brought you
to your second home.

Fellow Traveller 2

Laika, little lemon, little bug,
we should not have done it—we can say that, now.
Your death was unjustified: we did not learn
enough; one summer's day might have achieved
as much, one sunstruck car with the windows shut.

Dresses

It is time to launder dresses in Valivade;
a white-blonde, freckled orphan is playing mother
to a young girl old enough to be her sister.
One girl will wash the other's only dress
while the other waits, a nude Coppélia,
as like a child as a mannequin.

Irena gathers her limbs like kindling, perched
on the handlebars of a push-bike, dolly-light,
a cotton vulture knotted in her hair,
a matching dress sewn fast to the shape of the day
Marysia learned to make dresses in Valivade.

Tidiness

When I came to the sea I was clean as a sheet,
and, unsurprisingly, I had to swim
for miles before the smell of pink
and feathers left my fingertips for good.
The scent of having wanted to forget
is similar to though stronger by far
than the washed-out scent of what is now forgotten.
Enough of that: it's over now.
My shoulders gleam like copper pots;
my hair is stiff-peaked like a recipe.

Vection

Aniela, thinking herself returned
to the train in which her husband slept,
wept as one by a riverbank
when she saw his empty bunk and knew
for all her haste that she'd been still
and he long passed-away.

A student of the violin,
accustomed to her teacher's hands
positioning and repositioning
her stiff, wrong grip upon the bow,
flinches like a railway passenger
delivered from a dream of their own movement
when her teacher fumbles a phrase and holds
his careless fingers cold to her cheek
and tells her his fingers are cold.

Pink Postwar

The Pink Panther is in your bed again,
and he's cold as a scalded corpse.
His skin peels off like socks,
and he keeps on turning the lights out.
Ring for the help of a man in a hat;
he'll give you milk and empty all the lampshades
of hidden bottles labelled with kisses
and throw them to the dustbin. Cheers.

Had you not felt as tasering cold
the moment when you failed to notice him,
his wrong toes laid at the feet of your legs,
and taken a hot-water-bottle to bed
on a broom-handle, like a carrot and stick,
you would not have seen him shooting up
like an unexploded firework
and hopping a mad Krakowiak on burnt feet;
you would not be sitting sober now
and watching Pink purloin your sheets and pillows,
real as the tongue licking milk from your lips,
because he found no peace inside your house.

The Department of Sanitation van is riding
into the space in the sky reserved for sunsets.
Chase the dustman into the horizon.
Sleep until Pink has finished with your toothbrush.

Wesela (belonging to the wedding)

The night before the wedding, there was rain,
and lightning cracked the sky to adder skins;
the church wall gaped in badger-sized surprise,
and I dreamed of the Farthing Wood development,
the Scrabble set of bricks that made *our home*.
When morning sailed in like a yellow hat,
I stepped, in snapshots, from the wedding car—
a slow, white crumpling; my feet in their shoes
were slow, white shrews articulate with bows.
The cross-hatched hands of the parish priest were clasped
across a book in an indeterminate language.
Like the deft, uncouth reveal of an anagram,
the church doors opened, and I could have sworn
I saw a weasel dancing underneath
the seated *entrechats* of stockinged guests
whose shoes had such precisely-matching skirts
they seemed less real than the rabbits' panicking,
and when the weasel darted through my legs
and waited at my back to catch the flowers
I threw behind me, I was open-mouthed.
As two red foxes bounded through the graves
that lined the churchyard path, I thought I heard
an adder stirring in my lifted veil,
or maybe it was my forked tongue that thought,
all'sss well that endsss well, I sssuppose.

Sarah Jane's Geranium

It takes years, but the way you think of home
has been changing since the day you realised
that centuries of clutter in a box
too big to keep it in did not contain
a single potted plant to keep alive,
and brought aboard a pink geranium.
Some nights you think that home is relative
to time spent watering the same flower twice
a day, but other nights you lie awake
and think how different is a flower-pot
to flower-beds, and how, eventually,
the roots of something portable will bind
themselves into a white sandcastle and
demand a living-space as big outside
as it is in, and far less travel-sized.

土 *(Earth)*

This radical, with the addition of that for "heart," and the character for "hand" above it, means "strange," "unusual." It is used to convey the idea that the hand of the man working the earth transformed it.
  —*Understanding Chinese Characters: A Beginner's Guide to the Chinese Language*, Edoardo Fazzioli (trans. Geoffrey Culverwell)

屮 (SHOOT)

To leave one's own country,
one must first grow two shoots,
one on top of the other.

To be far from home, likewise,
one on top of the other,
one must first grow two shoots.

This is the hardest part.

豕 (PIG)

Take away the garden and
fatherland is family.

Take away the roof: suddenly family
puts its nose in the mud and will eat
the slop of the prodigal willingly.

Take away the roof: suddenly family
is terrible luck to any family
under whose roof it wanders uninvited.

田 (Rice Field)

To set your heart beneath a cultivated plot
is what it means to decide from now on
to observe the boundaries of your allotment.
Your husband calls you *żaba*, meaning 'frog',
as you move like a fond, sharp hen among your crops.
You think you will be buried near this spot.

木 (Tree)

To travel with a plum tree is a suitcase
in which you carry the fruit that is the thought
of a young boy sitting under a tree, a windfall
that heralds all those other suitcase trees
that are named for children's children under them.

Rochdale Nativity

And now she shows you New Jerusalem,
and by the cotton lungs of her bright wings
you see this mill town opening its gates
to these your daughters, who are jumping pearls,
each crowned alike in bliss and Bacofoil
and circling so fast their image blurs
like archive footage of a spinning frame.
You long to pray like her—your little queen,
her hands in easy worship, safe within
the tangibility of make-believe—
whose heart and soul are homophones reserved
for the mastery of second languages.
Across the stream that fathers cannot ford,
you send delighted ripples of applause.

Untied

When I came to the sea I was free as litter,
and, unsurprisingly, it sprouted wings
and scattered, screaming, into space
like fledgling stars in a creation myth.
I had done it before—had run to scare
the gulls from the shelled-out homes of hermit crabs
that marked the moonless line where sea meets shore.
I think there must be more to do than be
a scarecrow in the world—that is to say
to bury my brain in the road of a homesick girl.

Wycinanki (papercuts)

Woman without borders,
put down your shears and paper.
The flowers in your field are toothed like nettles.

I have loved you like a woman in a book
who suffered and can therefore do no wrong.
The flowers in your field are toothed like fishes,
and were they frogs, as their anthers are froghanded,
no bird in the forest would touch them.

The wind makes a scourge of spirits on the beach
like a vision of wolves in smoke;
all things that are capable of making
patterns are also capable of cruelty.
You live on the edge of an outer petal
placed on a map that is already busy with flowers.

Perdix (the partridge)

Provocative enough that he had left
his fish to waste upon the plate, but when
he left the artificer's table hyped
with its backbone reimagined in his grip,
claiming to have seen teeth and, furthermore,
to have invented something called the saw,
the children of necessity saw red.
They said, 'There's neither living man nor dead
will inhabit any home built up with beams
that are fashioned from their lives' uprooted trees
with your appropriation of a spine',
and cast him from the highest hill in town.

Athena, let him live with his mistakes
as I with mine; content him to be changed
into a bird that they can welcome, once
a year, in English, in pear trees, in song.

Lagan

i.m. Brian Ellis

Across the Sonoran desert, they piece together:
a happysnap, a plastic comb,
a hummingbird, a saint from out of town.
Deadman, your pockets are a tomb:
they spell the secrets of your birdpicked brains,
the blown electric fence behind your bones,
and who will answer when they telephone
the names that know your face behind the numbers?

My browneyed cousins, I have changed the weather:
your father's head is cocky as a jamjar
in a hat that has found its owner;
my fairhaired cousins, I have undiscovered
his favourite songs, his birthday in November,
the lagan of a life I don't remember.

Joy, in memoriam

after Afanasy Fet

I keep on greeting you, because the sun
has not stopped rising—it is rising still,
waking like a leaf in leaves that shake
with light—I'm here to tell you it is warm;

to tell you that the forest is awake
in every shoulder, every softening knee—
that it drinks in Spring from the anchors of its feet,
that the breath of birds stirs from their lifted cage;

to tell you I am passionate with waking,
that yesterday was not like yesterday,
and that my soul is tall with vertebrae—
that I am ready to be happy now;

to tell you that your having been awake
is with me everywhere, like a desire
to sing when the tip of the tongue is desolate
and songs mature like fruit trees in my mind.

Pyriform

i.m. Wiktor Juralewicz

Your youngest grandchild's pear tree is too young
to give her any fruit this year, but you
have hung its branches with elastic bands
and the lightbulb filaments of paperclips.
It's as though you had planned for her to paint them out—
as though the still life of her memory
would blaze your pear-shaped, bright ideas with light—
the garden and the tree and all your staging
background shadow, contrast, colourless,
the way the right Fresnel will isolate
the pool in which performances are lit
crisp as moons, whose gravity they say
was pondered in the context of the way
pomaceous fruit falls from pomaceous trees.

Vespertiliones

after Ovid

It is the beginning of the end. Still these working daughters,
storytellers all, spurn the terms of the feast of the god.
Suddenly drums, unapparent, stamping and raucous as horses,
clamour against the hollow piping of crooked instruments,
the tingling of coppers. The house is full of their storytellers' breath,
greater than faith, and something begins: their looms grow green,
the work of their hands works itself into the walls like ivy,
and where was once divinity, vines; where once the fraying
thread of fate, new shoots; tendrils of change emerge
from warp and weft, left, right, and centre, bear fruit.

They have spent the day like a useless coin; the time is coming
where light and dark cannot be told from dark and light,
a ticking, unnavigable country thunderous with unapparent borders.
The ceiling suddenly shakes overhead like a pane of glass;
it seems the house is glowing and flushed with a fire that flashes
and howls with the exorcisms of over-lingering spirits.
For what seems like the longest time the sisters are hidden in smoke;
there are many things that have burned, but they are only changing
to navigate the times. Their arms grow webs like looms,
featherless, instantly aerodynamic, a work of their hands;
they neither know nor care that they have lost their figures.
Nor do they fall or fly by their frills and furbelows,
maintained on wings that have no need of moon and sun.
Their voices are their bodies, their eyes, their ears, their maps;
they speak to find their way and, yes, they also complain.
By day, they slumber in eaves above the ceiling; evening
comes, a time they claim for new names of their own.

Medico della Peste

The plague doctor, whose mask
is a staple of the Carnival of Venice
when shining with metallic paint like a child's bicycle,

fills his leather beak
with clownishly unsubtle fragrances
strong enough to override the aromas of the dying.

It is like knowing everything
is frightening, and filling up your days
with cries of 'bird!' or 'baby bird!' or 'family of birds!',

determined to be a delighted
observer of fleeting things, clinging to them
as bees to lavender, exhausted boxers to punching bags.

A family of coots—
two masked adults, four putrid-looking chicks—
is swimming on the margins of your hometown's green canal;

the adults cannot see
the rotting figleaves of their bone-white feet
as they dive to fill their children's beaks, but of course their
    children can.

Later you decide
that knowing everything is frightening.
Your metaphor for selfless parenting—its testament

to histories like yours—
is not the half of it: apparently
the adult coot attacks its weakest chicks to stop their begging.

The plague doctor is
a symptom thought of as a harbinger
and masks himself against the symptoms rather than the cause;

the plague doctor is
nothing but a counter of the bodies
and could be anyone behind his shield of lavender.

Observe the Carnival
of Venice; read about its masks; decide
if *carnivalesque* is the term you would use for its anonymous chaos.

Think on the *larva*—the ghost—
who cannot eat; think on the *servetta muta,*
whose dark, round face is held in place with a bit that prevents her
    from speaking.

On Hosiery

for Aaron Smith

One history of silk would have us believe
a Chinese empress under a mulberry tree
once sat among the fruit of moths in making,
taking her tea, when one cocoon broke off, spiking
her drink with thread which unspooled easily
around a shortcut life of luxury.
It is elegant and boil-in-the-bag convenient—
believe no less romantic variant.

The silk moth is an unromantic thing:
its body is so heavy for its wings
that it is never destined to have flown,
regardless of permission to become.
Survive to hope: that your children die for something
with something to show for it—a pair of stockings
with which to love your love when the world is fucked
and women are drawing on seams and drawing them crooked;
that every damage done as though by moths
can be told as art or history or both.

At Easter, onionskins are boiled with eggs
in Polish homes; their shells, like English legs
in the gravy-painted, stocking-shortaged Blitz, are carved
with fierce tradition, varnished, saved
for future decoration; over time,
their innards shrink and clatter like cupped dice—
demo cocoons, percussive with dried larvae,
in tour-guides' hands in Chinese factories.

General note

On 10 February 1940, tens of thousands of Polish settlers and their families were taken from their homes in the Eastern Borderlands or *Kresy* of Poland and deported to Siberia. When the USSR joined the Allies, an 'amnesty' was agreed whereby the deported Poles either joined 'Anders' Army' or, in the case of the many women and children among them, were distributed amongst the various refugee camps of what were then the British colonies.

Many of those who had not already lost their lives to hunger and hard labour in the cold of Siberia now faced hunger and illness a second time along with the very real possibility of becoming separated from their families in a series of long, tortuous journeys from Siberia to the Middle East and beyond. Although this story is common to all four of my grandparents, it is the story of my then nine-year-old maternal grandmother, Maria Juralewicz (née Sztela), that informs the content of these poems.

Although she survived Siberia with her parents and two older siblings, her father later died on a train travelling to Orsk; she was separated from her mother in Bukhara and never saw her again. Her brother joined the cadets in Tehran, and from 1943 to 1948 she and her sister lived and were educated in a Polish orphanage and camp in Valivade, India. In 1948, she was brought to England with her sister and was reunited with her brother, who was later to emigrate to the USA.

She settled in Rochdale, where she became part of a thriving Polish community, married, had two children, and planted fruit trees for every one of her grandchildren. When she later wrote of her experiences as part of a larger project that was translated into English, her final words on the subject were, as ever, understated: 'How strange are the ups and downs of human destiny.'*

---

* Maria Juralewicz (Sztela), 'Osada Karłowicze, District Drohiczyn', in *Stalin's Ethnic Cleansing in Eastern Poland: Tales of the Deported 1940–1946*, ed. by Teresa Jeśmanowa, trans. by Eric J Whittle and Bronisława Kacperek (London: Association of the Families of the Borderland Settlers, 2000), pp. 558–561 (561).

Further notes

'Pisanki' is the Polish word for decorated Easter Eggs, derived from the word *pisać*, which in modern usage means 'to write'.

'Brother Staś' is based on Maria Juralewicz's verbal account of a brief separation from her siblings after having contracted typhoid in Tehran.

'Vection' is the word used to describe the sensation of having moved when in reality a large part of the visual field has moved—the feeling most commonly associated with railway passengers watching a neighbouring train pulling away and believing they are the ones who are moving.

'土 (Earth)' is based on Edoardo Fazzioli's *Understanding Chinese Characters: A Beginner's Guide to the Chinese Language*, translated into English by Geoffrey Culverwell. Each page of the book deals with a component of a character called a radical ('shoot', 'rice field', etc.) and gives examples of other characters composed from that radical. For instance, 'chū' (to go out, to produce) comprises the radical 'chě' (shoot) written twice, one above the other; when 'guó' (nation) is added to 'chū', it becomes 'chū guó' (to go abroad, to leave one's own country).*

'Wycinanki' refers to the art of Polish papercutting, traditionally with sheep-shears, and is heavily associated with Łowicz; Maria Juralewicz's mother was a native of the region.

'Perdix (the partridge)' refers to Daedalus's precocious nephew of the same name, who supposedly invented the saw, having drawn inspiration from a fish skeleton. Perdix was pushed from a great height—supposedly to his death—by his uncle, who was subsequently banished. On his way down, Perdix was transformed into a partridge by the goddess Athena.

'Lagan' is a nautical term for a type of shipwreck where goods cast overboard and sunk are tied to a floating marker and can later be reclaimed.

* Edoardo Fazzioli, *Understanding Chinese Characters: A Beginner's Guide to the Chinese Language*, trans. by Geoffrey Culverwell (London: Collins, 1987), p. 98.

Acknowledgements

To family and friends, thank you for everything.

Acknowledgements are due to the following publications in which some of these poems have appeared: *The Open Ear* and *The Lifeboat*.

Thanks to Stephen Connolly and Manuela Moser for *The Lifeboat*.

Special thanks must go to Joe Lines and Padraig Regan, whose boundless capacity for constructive criticism has been nothing short of astonishing.

To anyone who has ever read, workshopped, edited, or otherwise cast a critical eye over any one of my poems, thank you for making them better.

I owe a great deal of gratitude to Bernard O'Donoghue, who took on the task of introducing a pamphlet whose historical context is both complex and not widely known with benevolent elegance and apparent ease; his reading of the pamphlet is one to which it aspires. His tutorials on Brian Friel quite literally changed my life.

Emma and Rachel, thank you for this pamphlet and for your press.

To my Dad (who didn't like poetry), thank you for reading my poems anyway.

To my Babcia, for her life and for the impact it had on mine, all my love and thanks.

About the poet

Zosia Kuczyńska was born in Solihull in 1988 and grew up in Nottingham, where she is currently a Teaching Affiliate at the University of Nottingham. She has recently completed her doctorate on 'Time and Space in the Plays of Brian Friel' at Trinity College Dublin and has had poems published in *The Open Ear* and with *The Lifeboat*.